WORDS TO LIVE BY

Nahm-Sheik Park

국제영어대학원대학교 출판부
INTERNATIONAL GRADUATE SCHOOL OF ENGLISH PRESS

WORDS TO LIVE BY

Nahm-Sheik Park

국제영어대학원대학교 출판부
INTERNATIONAL GRADUATE SCHOOL OF ENGLISH PRESS

Contents

Preface

The 150-odd bite-size nuggets of wisdom presented in this volume represent part of the maxims that I have already shared, on-line, with the members of the IGSE family over the last two years. I have decided to use these same sayings to reach out, off-line, to all Korean lovers of English in hopes of adding to the fertility of English-language soil in Korea.

The proverbs in question have proven to be instrumental in forging solid ties that bind the whole IGSE family closer together. My hope is that they also serve the larger purpose of providing a new way for Korea's English-language aficionados outside IGSE to renew and deepen their affinity for the language as well as the culture that underlies it.

Each of the maxims featured in the booklet is followed by interpretive commentary and a few bilingual notes, which are by no means meant to be exhaustive. Oftentimes, annotation is precluded for space reasons even where it would seem to be more needed than not. On the other hand, some of the notes that do appear may be thought of as mere space-filling "ballast" of sorts.

Incidentally, this booklet is my way of helping introduce IGSE to Korean society at large. IGSE is the only ELT-specific school in Korea today. IGSE is the one and only graduate school of its kind in present-day Korea, catering exclusively to the advancement of English-language teaching. I have no reservation whatsoever in calling IGSE the face of advanced studies for wave upon wave of future Korean teachers of English. I dedicate this small collection of maxims to IGSE and the rest of the Korean ELT community.

Before I conclude, I would like to acknowledge my debt to some of my friends, who have had a hand in making it easier for me to put together this labor of love. Let me especially single out Ms. Jungmin Choi and Professor Young-Woo Kim, both of IGSE, for their constant moral support and priceless editorial advice.

Nahm-Sheik Park
IGSE (International Graduate School of English)
Seoul

1

The first blow is half the battle.

"Well begun is half done" says about the same thing. Capsules of wisdom such as this can add quite a bit to our English-language repertoire.

*capsule: 캡슐 / *quite a bit: 많이 / *repertoire: 레퍼토리

2

When the cat's away, the mice will play.

The absence of an authority figure often gives rise to discipline issues, doesn't it? Note here that "away" and "play" rhyme, which can serve as a mnemonic aid.

*authority figure: 힘있는 사람 / *give rise to discipline issues: 규율상의 문제가 생기게 하다 / *mnemonic aid: 기억을 돕는 장치

3

Burn not your house to fright the mouse away.

You wouldn't opt for overly extreme measures, would you? As they say, "Moderation in all things." Note that "house" and "mouse" rhyme here.

*fright: 놀라게 하다, frighten의 옛말 / *opt for overly extreme measures: 지나치게 과도한 조처를 선택하다 / *moderation: 중용

4

Physician, heal thyself.

Based on Luke 4:23, this proverb warns against being (too) critical of other people.

*Physician, heal thyself: 의사 선생님, 당신 자신의 병이나 치료하시지요 / *Luke 4:23: 누가 복음 4장 23절 / *be critical of X: X를 비판하다

5

Garbage in, garbage out.

This computer-age proverb is often boiled down to the acronym GIGO, pronounced "guy go." The basic message here is that faulty data fed into a computer will only lead to distorted information.

*be boiled down to X: X로 축약되다 / *faulty data fed into a computer: 컴퓨터에 입력된 잘못된 자료 / *distorted: 왜곡된

6

Bacchus has drowned more men than Neptune.

This proverb says that drinking has claimed more lives than drowning, the warning here being against drinking to excess. In case you didn't know, Bacchus is the god of wine and Neptune the god of the sea.

*claim more lives: 더 많은 목숨을 앗아가다/ *drinking to excess: 과음, 지나친 음주 / *In case you didn't know: (아직) 모르고 있다면

7

Greedy eaters dig their graves with their teeth.

This proverb is about the danger of excessive eating. "Many dishes make many diseases" makes a similar point.

*greedy: 지나치게 욕심 많은, 탐욕스러운 / *excessive: 과도한 / *Many dishes make many diseases: 음식을 많이 먹으면 병이 많이 생긴다

8

Too much of aught is good for naught.

If in excess, even the best of things may be harmful. "Aught" and "naught" are old-fashioned words for "anything" and "nothing," respectively.

*If in excess: 과도하면, 지나치면 / *even the best of things: 아무리 좋은 것이라도 / *respectively: 각각

9

Beauty is in the eye of the beholder.

The point here is that beauty is a matter of (subjective) opinion. Note here that both "beauty" and "beholder" begin with /b/. Examples of alliteration such as this may be of some mnemonic help.

*be in the eye of beholder: 보는 사람의 눈에 따라 다르다 / *be a matter of (subjective) opinion: 주관적인 판단에 달려 있다 / *alliteration: 두운

10

Birth is much, but breeding is more.

The implication here is that the way we are born is important, but how we are bred is even more important. Note the alliteration involving three tokens of /b/ and two of /m/.

*breeding: 양육, 교육 / *implication: 함축된 의미 / *involving three tokens of X: X 셋을 포함하는

11

Honey catches more flies than vinegar.

Gentleness is often more persuasive than harshness. "Kindness is the noblest weapon to conquer with" also speaks to the power of gentleness.

*vinegar: 식초 / *persuasive: 설득력이 있는 / *harshness: 가혹함, 혹독함 / *the noblest weapon to conquer with: 정복을 위한 가장 고상한 무기 / *speak to the power of gentleness: 온화함의 힘을 취급하다

12

The noblest vengeance is to forgive.

There is an ennobling quality to forgiveness, right? Also preaching forgiveness are "Forgive and forget" and "Let bygones be bygones."

*vengeance: 복수, 앙갚음 / *ennobling quality: 품위를 높여주는 자질 / *preach: 설교하다 / *Let bygones be bygones: 과거는 과거로 묻어 버리자

13

Variety is the spice of life.

Addressed here is the delectable quality of change. Making a similar point is "A change is as good as a rest."

*Variety is the spice of life.: 변화가 인생의 양념이다 / *Addressed here is X: 여기서 다루는 주제는 X이다 / *delectable: 유쾌한, 즐거움을 주는

14

If you would be well served, serve yourself.

The suggestion is that relying on other people is not the way to get things done well. Making a point along similar lines is "If you want a thing well done, do it yourself."

*be well served: 대우를 잘 받다, be treated well / *a point along similar lines: a similar point / *If you want a thing well done: 일이 잘 되기를 원하거든

15

Better an apple given than eaten.

The same thing is preached in "It is more blessed to give than to receive" (Acts 20:35).

*Better an apple given than eaten: 사과는 자신이 먹는 것보다 남에게 주는 것이 더 좋다 / *blessed: 축복을 받은 / *Acts 20:35: 사도행전 20장 35절, Acts = Acts of the Apostles

16

Never say die.

About the virtue of perseverance, this proverb says never to give up. "If at first you don't succeed, try, try, try again" sends a similar message.

*Never say die: 죽는(다는) 소리하지 말라, 포기하지 말라 / *the virtue of perseverance: 인내의 미덕 / *try, try, try again: 몇 번이고 되풀이해 시도하다

17

A blind man may sometimes hit the mark.

Being about dumb luck, this proverb may be used when something good gets done all by accident.

*hit the mark: 표적에 명중하다 / *dumb luck: 뜻밖의 행운 / *X gets done all by accident: 뜻밖에 X를 해내다

18

Never do things by halves.

The counsel here is to approach whatever we do full of passion. Doing things halfheartedly won't cut it, will it?

*by halves: 온전치 않게, 불완전하게 / *counsel: 충언, 권고 / *approach X full of passion: 충만한 열정을 가지고 X에 임하다 / *Doing things halfheartedly won't cut it: 마지못해 일하는 것으로는 안 된다

19

From hearing comes wisdom; from speaking, repentance.

So we should keep from talking too much, shouldn't we? An essentially identical piece of advice is found in "Hear much, speak little."

*repentance: 후회 / *keep from doing X: X를 하는 것을 피하다 / *essentially: 근본적으로

20

In haste is error.

The advice here is not to rush things. "Hasty work, double work" seems to strike a similar note.

*rush things: 일을 서두르다 / *Hasty work, double work: 일을 서두르면, 일을 두 번 하게 된다 / *strike a similar note: 비슷한 내용의 말을 하다

21

If the shoe fits, wear it.

We are advised here to be accepting of even unpleasant things said about us should they be justified." British English often uses "cap" for "shoe" here.

*If the shoe fits, wear it: 신발이 맞으면, 신으라 / *be accepting of X: X를 받아 들이다, X를 인정하다 / *should they be justified: if they should be justified, 정당한 이유가 있다면

22

One hour today is worth two tomorrow.

We are counseled here not to put things off till another day. Similar advice is given in "One of these days is none of these days." Note that this latter proverb resorts to a bunch of rhyme and alliteration.

*counsel: 권고하다, 충언하다 / *put things off till X: 일을 X까지 미루다 / *resort to a bunch of X: 일단의 X를 사용하다

23

It is easy to be wise after the event.

The focus here is on the clarity of hindsight (and the futility thereof.) A similar sentiment shows up in "If things were to be done twice, all would be wise."

*after the event: 사후에, 어떤 사건이 일어난 다음에 / *the clarity of hind-sight: 과거에 대한 판단의 극명함 / *the futility thereof: 그것의 쓸모 없음

24

What can't be cured must be endured.

The message here has to do with the necessity of endurance in a trying stretch of time when things are (almost) impossible to put up with.

*have to do with X: X와 관계되다 / *necessity of endurance: 인내의 필요성 / *trying stretch of time: 고통스러운 시기 / *impossible to put up with: (도저히) 참을 수 없는

25

Fish and guests smell in three days.

The implication here is that we must not overstay our welcome. A similar point is made in "Do not wear out your welcome."

*Fish and guests smell in three days: 생선과 손님은 3일이면 (썩은) 냄새가 난다 / *overstay one's welcome: 환영을 받지 못할 때까지 머무르다 / *wear out one's welcome: overstay one's welcome

26

The grass is always greener on the other side of the fence.

Implied here is the discontent that we often experience with our lot relative to that of other people.

*on the other side of the fence: 울타리 다른 편에(서), 이웃집에(서) / *discontent: 불만족 / *our lot relative to that of other people: 다른 사람과 비교한 우리의 상황

27

Half a loaf is better than no bread.

It says here that we should be grateful for what we currently have no matter how little it may be. "Something is better than nothing" is another way of saying essentially the same thing.

*half a loaf: (빵) 반 덩어리 / *be grateful for X: X에 감사하다 / *currently: 지금, 현재

28

You win some, you lose some.

The main point here is that we can't always succeed and that failure is a fact of life. Success and failure may be nextdoor neighbors. "You can't win them all" says about the same thing.

*be a fact of life: 인생의 현실 / *nextdoor neighbor: 바로 이웃, 이웃 사촌 / *You can't win them all: 모든 것을 다 잘할 수는 없다

29

Brevity is the soul of wit.

We are counseled here to refrain from saying too much. "The fewer the words, the better the prayer" delivers a similar message.

*Brevity is the soul of wit: 간결이 재치의 핵심이다 / *We are counseled here to do X: 이는 우리들에게 X를 하라는 권고이다 / *refrain from saying too much: 말을 많이 하는 것을 삼가다

30

Speak well of your friend; of your enemy, say nothing.

What is suggested here is that speaking ill of our enemies is not the way to handle them.

*speak well of X: X를 좋게 말하다 / *speak ill of X: X를 나쁘게 말하다 / *be not the way to handle X: X를 다루는 옳은 방법이 아니다

31

The nearest way is commonly the foulest.

The moral here is that shortcuts are not necessarily economical. Also warning against cutting corners is "The longest way around is the shortest way home."

*moral: 교훈 / *shortcuts are not necessarily economical: 지름길이 꼭 경제적인 것은 아니다 / *warn against cutting corners: 쉬운 길(만)을 가려 하지 말도록 경고하다

32

The best things are hard to come by.

The point here is that we must keep on pursuing our goal no matter what. "Things that are hard to come by are much set by" is also about the importance of perseverance.

*be hard to come by: 구하기 힘들다 / *keep on pursuing our goal: 우리의 목표를 향하여 매진하다 / *no matter what: 무슨 일이 있어도 / *be much set by: 높이 평가되다 / *perseverance: 인내, 참고 견딤

33

If a thing is worth doing, it is worth doing well.

We are reminded here of the value of seeing things through as long as they are deserving.

*be worth doing (well): (잘) 할 가치가 있다 / *see things through: 시작한 일을 끝까지 해내다 / *as long as they are deserving: 가치가 있는 일이라면

34

Self-praise stinks.

This proverb also takes the form "A man's praise in his own mouth stinks." Delivering a similar moral is "Self-praise is no recommendation."

*Self-praise stinks: 자화자찬은 역겹다 / *one's praise in one's own mouth: one's self praise, 자화자찬 / *recommendation: 추천

35

Deliver your words not by number but by weight.

"Few words are best" is another way of saying about the same thing. "Brevity is the soul of wit" also delivers a similar message. We should, indeed, always weigh our words carefully.

*Deliver your words: 말을 하다 / *not by number but by weight: 수량이 아니라 비중으로 / *weigh one's words: 할 말을 심사 숙고하다

36

Better pass a danger once than be always in fear.

The advice here is not to be too afraid of things that may stand in our way.

*pass a danger: 위험한 고비를 넘기다 / *be in fear: 무서워하다 / *stand in our way: 방해가 되다, 길목을 막다

37

When one door shuts, another opens.

We should cheer up no matter how disappointing things may be. "Look on the bright side" says about the same thing.

*cheer up: 힘내다 / *disappointing: 실망스러운 / *Look on the bright side: (상황의) 밝은 면을 보라

38

Empty vessels make the greatest sound.

The implication here is that foolish people tend to be talkative. "Shallow streams make the most din" says about the same thing.

*empty vessel: 빈 그릇 / *tend to be talkative: 말이 많은 경향이 있다 / *Shallow streams make the most din: 얕은 시냇물이 가장 요란하다

39

We are not born for ourselves.

We shouldn't be too selfish, should we? "Who eats his cock alone must saddle his horse alone" also delivers a sermon against selfishness.

*saddle one's horse: 말에 안장을 얹다 / *deliver a sermon against X: X가 좋지 않다는 설교를 하다

40

No bees, no honey; no work, no money.

We are reminded here that diligence is at the heart of a good work ethic and is sure to be rewarded.

*diligence is at the heart of X: 근면이 X의 핵심이다 / *a good work ethic: 좋은 근무 태도 / *be sure to be rewarded: 꼭 보상을 받다

41

Better the devil you know than the devil you don’t know.

The message here is that we should be wary of making (sudden) changes, as by reversing course.

*Better the devil you know than the devil you don't know.: 구관이 명관이다 / *be wary of X: X를 경계하다 / *reverse course: 가던 길과 반대 방향으로 가다, 정반대 방향을 택하다

42

Of thy sorrow, be not too sad; of thy joy, be not too glad.

Surely, publicly venting our emotions, of either joy or sorrow, is not exactly the best way to handle them.

*publicly venting our emotions: 공개적으로 감정을 드러내다

43

Every man is the architect of his own fortune.

It says here that everyone is responsible for their own destiny. So why don't we aim high and give our all to our aspirations whatever they may be?

*architect of one's own fortune: 자기 운명의 설계자 / *responsible for one's own destiny: 자신의 운명에 책임을 지다 / *aim high: 목표를 높이 세우다 / *give our all to our aspirations: 우리의 갈망을 향하여 최선을 다하다

44

He that follows nature is never out of his way.

We disobey nature in so many ways and suffer the consequences thereof. We use chemically processed products on a daily basis. This may often be to blame for birth defects, cancer and such.

*suffer the consequences thereof: 그 결과로 생긴 고통을 겪다 / *chemically processed: 화학적으로 처리된 / *and such: 등등

45

Learn young, learn fair.

This is about youth being the ideal time to learn things. Delivering a similar message is "What's learnt in the cradle lasts till the tomb."

*Learn young, learn fair: 어려서 배우면, 잘 배운다 / *What is learnt in the cradle: 요람에서 배운 것 / *lasts till the tomb: 무덤까지 간다

46

Life is short and time is swift.

This is about the brevity of life. "Life is half spent before we know what it is" also is about the transient nature of our sojourn on this planet.

*swift: 빠른 / *transient: 덧없는, 순간 지나가 버리는 / *our sojourn on this planet: 이 행성(지구)에서의 우리들의 체류

47

Many a little makes a mickle.

Little things do add up, don't they? "Mickle" here is an old-fashioned word for "much." "Many drops make a shower" also makes the point that every little helps.

*Little things do add up: 조그만 것들도 합하면 큰 것이 된다 / *Many drops make a shower: 빗방울도 많이 모이면 소나기가 된다

48

He that falls today may rise tomorrow.

The spirit of optimism encouraged here is also found in "Look on the bright side" and "When one door shuts, another opens."

*(the spirit of) optimism: 낙천주의 (정신) / *encourage: 권장하다, 고무하다

49

A man's studies pass into his character.

Our knowledge (or education) helps shape who we are. Don't you think?

*studies: 공부, 수학, 학업 / *pass into his character: 인격으로 녹아 들어 가다 / *help shape X: X의 형성에 도움이 되다

50

When fortune smiles, embrace her.

We must make sure not to miss an opportunity when one comes our way, right? Making a similar pitch is "Opportunity seldom knocks twice."

*When fortune smiles, embrace her: 행운의 여신이 미소하거든, 그녀를 껴안으라 / *come our way: 우리 쪽으로 오다 / *make a similar pitch: 비슷한 내용을 말하다 / *seldom knocks twice: 두 번 노크하는 일은 거의 없다

51

The tortoise wins the race while the hare is sleeping.

Based on one of Aesop's fables, this proverb is about the value of perseverance.

*tortoise: 거북이 / *hare: 산토끼 / *fable: 우화

52

Willows are weak, yet they bind other wood.

"Weak things united become strong" is a more direct way of saying the same thing.

*Willows are weak: 버드나무는 약하다 / *yet they bind other wood: 그러나 그것은 다른 나무를 묶는다 / *Weak things united become strong: 약한 것들도 하나로 뭉치면 강해진다

53

Nothing is impossible to a willing heart.

"Where there is a will, there is a way" delivers a similar message. We can get just about anything done as long as our will is there.

*willing heart: 기꺼이 하고자 하는 마음(을 가진 사람) / *Where there is a will: (하려는) 의지가 있는 곳에 / *there is a way: 길이 있다 / *as long as our will is there: 우리들이 그렇게 할 의지가 있는 한

54

By writing, you learn to write.

The message here is that experience in writing is the best teacher of writing. "By speaking, you learn to speak" would be a good answer to "How can we get a good command of spoken English?"

*By writing, you learn to write: 글을 직접 써봐야, 글쓰기를 배우게 된다 / *get a good command of X: X를 통달하다

55

The world is for him who has patience.

It is suggested here that patience always pays off. "Patient men win the day" says about the same thing.

*patience: 인내심 / *pay off: 좋은 결과를 가져오다 / *Patient men win the day: 인내심이 있는 사람이 (결국) 승자가 된다

56

The longest day has an end.

Everything, no matter how taxing, is bound to come to an end. Saying the same thing is "The longest night will have an end." Buck up, folks.

*taxing: 힘이 드는, 부담이 되는 / *be bound to come to an end: 끝장나게 마련이다 / *Buck up, folks: 여러분, 힘내세요

57

The darkest hour is that before the dawn.

The point here is that we should not take a dim view of life no matter how grim things may seem. A similar point is made in "After a storm comes a calm."

*dawn: 여명, 새벽 / *take a dim view of X: X를 비관적/회의적으로 보다 / *grim: 냉혹한 / *calm: 고요(함)

58

Good to begin well; better to end well.

A good beginning is important, but even more important is a good ending. That being the case, we must always remember to finish what we start and do it well.

*even more important: 그보다 더 중요한 (것은) / *That being the case: 그러므로, 그러한 것이 사실이므로 / *remember to do X: X를 하도록 명심하다

59

Faith will move mountains.

This is about the power of faith. "He can who believes he can" makes a similar point.

*faith: 믿음 / *He can who believes he can: 할 수 있다고 믿는 사람은 할 수 있다

60

The journey of a thousand miles begins with a single step.

This is an English version of 천리 길도 한 걸음부터. "The first blow is half the battle" also emphasizes the value of the first step.

*journey: 여행 / *an English version of X: X의 영어판 / *The first blow is half the battle: 첫 타격이 싸움의 반은 된다

61

March winds and April showers bring forth May flowers.

The kind of inclement weather Britain normally gets in March and April may, indeed, be the harbinger of the beautiful spring flowers it gets in May.

*bring forth X: X를 가져 오다 / *inclement: 험악한, 매우 궂은 / *harbinger of X: 전령, 선구자

62

Plan the whole year in the spring.

This is an English version of an old Chinese saying. The message here may be that a project needs to be well planned at the very beginning.

*Plan the whole year in the spring: 일년 전체를 봄에 계획하라 / *X needs to be well planned: X를 잘 계획할 필요가 있다 / *at the very beginning: 최초에, 맨 처음부터

63

Repentance comes too late.

It is often too late by the time we come to regret something. For example, we often regret not having done enough for our loved ones while they were still with us on Planet Earth.

*repentance: 후회 / *regret: 뉘우치다, 후회하다 / *Planet Earth: 행성 지구

64

Grief is lessened when imparted to others.

Striking a similar note is "A cure for all sorrows is conversation."

*Grief is lessened: 슬픔이 줄어든다 / *when imparted to others: 그것을 남에게 하소연하고 나면 / *Striking a similar note is X: X도 비슷한 내용의 말이다

65

The race is not to the swift, nor the battle to the strong.

Based on Ecclesiastes 9:11, this proverb speaks to the importance of perseverance.

*The race is not to the swift: 빠르다고 경주에 이기는 것이 아니다 / *nor the battle to the strong: 힘세다고 싸움에 이기는 것도 아니다 / *Based on Ecclesiastes 9:11: (구약) 전도서 9장 11절에 근거한

66

Easier said than done.

Things are indeed (far) easier said than done. "From word to deed is a great space" also speaks to the huge gap (or chasm) between words and deeds.

*Easier said than done: 말하기는 행동하기 보다 쉽다 / *From word to deed is a great space: 말과 행동 사이에 큰 차이가 있다 / *chasm between words and deeds: 말과 행동 사이의 (큰) 간격

67

Laugh and the world laughs with you; weep and you weep alone.

The point here is that looking on the bright side trumps looking on the dark side. They also say "Laughter is the best medicine."

*look on the bright side: 밝은 면을 보다 / *look on the dark side: 어두운 면을 보다 / *X trumps Y: X가 Y보다 낫다, X가 Y를 이기다

68

Preserve the old, but know the new.

An English version of 온고지신, this proverb says to strike a balance between the old and the new. The wisdom is especially applicable to our quest for knowledge.

*preserve the old: 옛 것을 보존하다 / *strike a balance between X and Y: X와 Y사이에 균형을 취하다 / *applicable to our quest for knowledge: 우리들의 지식추구에 적용될 수 있는

69

An oak is not felled at one stroke.

Attaining a lofty goal is an incremental, painstaking process. "Rome was not built in a day" makes about the same point.

*An oak is not felled at one stroke: 참나무는 한번 찍어서 넘어뜨릴 수 없다 / *attain a lofty goal: 지고한 목표를 성취하다 / *an incremental, painstaking process: 점진적이고 힘이 드는

70

Better ask the way than go astray.

Something like 아는 길도 물어 가라, this proverb underscores the wisdom of asking for help and direction from those who know more than we do.

*go astray: 정도에서 벗어나다 / *underscore X: X를 강조하다 / *ask for help and direction: 도움과 안내를 요청하다

71

Every cloud has a silver lining.

It says here that nothing can be all bad. A similar point is made in "Look on the bright side" and "When one door shuts, another opens."

*silver lining: 은으로 된 안감, 은으로 된 알맹이 / *nothing can be all bad: 뭐이든 모두가 나쁠 수는 없다

72

Flesh is frail.

How true! All humans are so weak and vulnerable. "Men are not angels" expresses a similar sentiment.

*Flesh is frail: 육신은 약하다, 인간은 약하다 / *vulnerable: 약한, 취약한

73

Failure teaches success.

Failure often is the mother of success, right? At any rate, "You can't win them all." So you might as well accept failure as a fact of life and use it as motivation to take whatever you do to another level.

*might as well do X: 하는 편이 낫다 / *motivation: 동기 / *take X to another level: X를 한 차원 상승시키다

74

The best things come in small packages.

Precious things like diamond rings come in small packages, right? You may find yourself vertically challenged, for example, but you can rank right up there with the brightest people in the world.

*vertically challenged: 키가 작은 / *rank right up there with Xs: X들과 겨루다, X들과 어깨를 나란히 하다

75

Don't change horses in midstream.

We are warned here against making changes in midcourse. A similar message is conveyed in "A tree often transplanted bears not much fruit."

*in midstream: while crossing a stream, (물을 건너는) 도중에 / *in mid-course: 도중에 / *A tree often transplanted: 나무를 자주 옮겨 심으면 / *bears not much fruit: 열매를 많이 맺지 못한다

76

Use legs and have legs.

The point here is that using your legs is the best way to increase their value as a tool of locomotion. The same goes for your English. Use English constantly and you will have your English.

*a tool of locomotion: 이동의 수단 / *The same goes for X: X도 마찬가지다 / *constantly: 항시, 끊임없이

77

Pride goes before a fall.

The admonition here is to guard against excessive pride. Aren't we being a bit too complacent about our competence from time to time?

*admonition: 훈계 / *guard against excessive pride: 지나친 자존심을 경계하다 / *complacent: 자만심을 가진

78

You can't have it both ways.

This is about the necessity of making a clear choice when confronted with two equally enticing alternatives.

*You can't have it both ways: 두 가지를 다 가질 수 없다, 양자택일해야 한다 / *when confronted with X: X에 직면할 경우 / *two equally enticing alternatives: 똑같이 마음을 끄는 두 가지 가능성들

79

Nothing seek, nothing find.

This proverb is about the value of aspiring to an ambitious goal. A similar point is made in "Nothing crave, nothing have."

*Nothing seek, nothing find: 아무것도 추구하지 않으면, 아무것도 얻을 수 없다 / *aspire to X: X를 향하여 갈망하다/ *Nothing crave: 아무것도 갈망하지 않으면

80

Medicines are not meat to live by.

The warning here is that medicines are not to be consumed the way food is. We need to think twice before we turn to things like pain relievers and anti-biotics, which many of us do on a daily basis.

*meat to live by: 일용할 양식, 일상 먹고 사는 음식 / *be consumed: 먹다, 소비되다 / *pain relievers and antibiotics: 진통제와 항생제

81

The mouth is the executioner and the doctor of the body.

We are reminded here that a proper, balanced diet is of great importance to our health. Literally interpreted, the proverb says that our diet will either kill or cure us.

*executioner: 사형 집행인 / *proper, balanced diet: 적절하고 균형있는 음식 / *Literally interpreted: 문자 그대로 해석하면

82

He who drinks a little too much drinks much too much.

Alcohol is to be consumed in moderate amounts only, right? A similar piece of advice may apply to food consumption as well: "He who eats a little too much eats much too much."

*is to be consumed: 먹어야 한다, 마셔야 한다, 소비되어야 한다 / *in moderate amounts: 적당한 양으로 / *consumption: 소비

83

Constant dripping wears away the stone.

"Step after step, the ladder is ascended" makes a similar point.

*Constant dripping wears away the stone: 계속 떨어지는 물방울은 돌도 닳아 없앤다. / *Step after step, the ladder is ascended: 사닥다리는 한 계단씩 차근차근 오른다

84

Temperance is the best physic.

We are told here that sensible management of how we live is the key to good health. Parenthetically, "physic" is a rather old-fashioned word for "medicine."

*Temperance is the best physic: 절제가 가장 좋은 약이다 / *sensible management: 사리에 맞는 관리 / *parenthetically: 덧붙여 말하자면

85

The blood of the soldier makes the glory of the general.

Originating in the business of soldiering, this proverb is about what teamwork is all about, that is, the teamwork of soldier/follower and commander/leader.

*the glory of the general: 장군의 영광 / *is about what teamwork is all about: 조직생활이 어떤 것인지에 관한 것이다 / *soldiering: 군대 생활, 조직의 대원으로서 하는 생활

86

Solitude is often the best society.

Solitude is better than bad company, for example. As they say, "Better be alone than in bad company."

*solitude: 홀로 있음, 고독 / *is often the best society: 고독은 흔히 가장 좋은 벗이다 / *(in) bad company: 나쁜 사람(과 함께)

87

Sickness shows us what we are.

In the face of sickness, we are all so helpless. The strongest of humans are but humans.

*Sickness shows us what we are: 병에 걸리면 인간이 어떤 존재인가가 들어난다 / *In the face of sickness: 아픔에 직면하면 / *helpless: 무기력한, 전혀 힘을 못 쓰는 / *The strongest of humans are but humans: 아무리 강한 사람도 사람에 불과하다

88

A soft answer turns away wrath.

A soft answer is indeed a good antidote to anger.

*soft answer: 부드러운 대답 / *turn away wrath: 노여움을 물리치다 / *anti-dote to anger: 노여움을 삭이는 해독제

89

Truth and oil are ever above.

Truth is impossible to suppress, so it is no use trying to conceal it. "Truth will out" makes the same point.

*ever above: 항시 위로 떠 오르는 / *suppress: 억누르다 / *it is no use trying to conceal it: 그것을 숨기려 해도 소용없다/ *Truth will out: 진실은 밝혀지게 마련이다

90

Sleep is better than medicine.

Sleep is indeed a key to health. We would do well to make sure that sleep deprivation is not too much of an issue for us.

*would do well to make sure: 확실히 하는 것이 좋다 / *sleep deprivation: 수면 결핍 / *be not too much of an issue: 별 문제가 안되다

91

Friends are made in wine and proved in tears.

The suggestion here is that "foul-weather" friends, as opposed to mere "fair-weather" friends, are the best of friends. In other words, "A friend in need is a friend indeed."

*in tears: 눈물을 흘리면서, 어려운 가운데 / *foul-weather friends: 어려울 때의 친구 / *as opposed to fair-weather friends: 아무런 문제도 없을 때의 친구에 반해서

92

He that eats least eats most.

The advice here is to eat sparingly. Remember "Greedy eaters dig their graves with their teeth." "Less is more" apparently applies to eating as well.

*sparingly: 조금씩, 아끼면서 / *greedy: 탐욕스러운 / *Less is more: (보다) 작은 것이 (보다) 큰 것이다

93

It will all come right in the wash.

"It will all come out in the wash" is another version of this proverb. "There is a good time coming" also means that things will improve.

*come right in the wash: 결국 좋은 결과가 나오다 / *There is a good time coming: 앞으로 좋은 때가 온다

94

A hedge between keeps friendship green.

We are reminded here of the need to always respect privacy, even in our dealings with our (closest) friends. We must always be careful not to pry into the personal affairs of other people.

*hedge (between): 울타리 / *respect privacy: 프라이버시를 존중하다 / *dealings: 교제, 관계, 거래 / *pry into X: X를 꼬치꼬치 캐다

95

Spend not where you may save; spare not where you must spend.

The advice here has to do with how to best handle our resources, especially our financial resources.

*spare: 아끼다 / *have to do with X: X와 관련되다 / *(financial) resources: (금전적) 자산

96

The lower millstone grinds as well as the upper.

This is about all humans being equal, be they great or lowly. "Every groom is a king at home" says about the same thing.

*the lower millstone: 맷돌의 하단 / *the upper: the upper millstone, 맷돌의 상단 / *lowly: 비천한, 신분이 낮은 / *groom: 말을 다루는 사람, 말구종

97

Have but few friends, though many acquaintances.

This is about the wisdom of exercising special care in choosing who to be friends with. As they say, "A friend to everybody is a friend to nobody."

*but few friends: only few friends, 친구는 몇몇만 / *though many acquaintances: 지인은 많지만 / *exercise special care: 특별히 주의하다

98

Meat is much, but manners is more.

Politeness, as manifested in good manners, is of great value, in fact, even more so than (good) food. Note the alliteration here, involving four tokens of /m/.

*meat: 먹을 것, 음식 / *as manifested in X: X에 나타나는 것과 같은

99

Mercy surpasses justice.

Forgiveness is so ennobling that it outshines justice. Given this message, shouldn't we always forgive other people? They say "The noblest vengeance is to forgive."

*Mercy surpasses justice: 자비가 정의를 능가한다 / *X outshines Y: X가 Y보다 빛난다 / *Given this message: 이러한 뜻을 감안하면 / *The noblest vengeance is to forgive: 가장 고상한 보복은 용서이다

100

He who would climb the ladder must begin at the bottom.

We are reminded here of how very important patience is, especially when seeking to attain an ambitious goal.

*climb the ladder: 사닥다리를 오르다 / *begin at the bottom: 맨 아래에서 시작하다 / *seek to attain X: X를 이루려고 노력하다

101

Small is the seed of every greatness.

A similar sentiment is expressed in the more folksy "Every oak has been an acorn."

*Small is the seed of every greatness: 모든 위대함은 조그만 씨로부터 나온다 / *folksy: 토속적인, 친근한 / *Every oak has been an acorn: 모든 큰 나무도 조그만 씨에서 나온다

102

Hitch your wagon to a star.

This saying, due to Ralph Waldo Emerson (1803-1882), urges us to be ambitious. "Aim high" says about the same thing in plainer English.

*Hitch your wagon to a star: 마차를 별에 묶으라 / *due to Ralph Waldo Emerson: Ralph Waldo Emerson이 한 말로서 / *urge X to do Y: X에게 Y하기를 역설하다 / *in plainer English: 보다 쉬운 말로 표현하여

103

Times change and we with them.

Everything in the world is bound to change over time. Lest we be left behind, we must keep abreast of the changing times.

*be bound to change over time: 시간이 흐르면 바뀌게 마련이다 / *Lest we be left behind: 뒤지지 않기 위해서 / *keep abreast of X: X와 어깨를 나란히 하다, X에 뒤지지 않고 따라가다

104

"After you" is good manners.

Thinking of other people ahead of ourselves is good manners. Besides, putting other people's interests above our own can make everyone happier.

*"After you" is good manners: 양보하는 것이 좋은 예절이다 / *ahead of X: X에 우선하여, X보다 먼저 / *put X above Y: X를 Y보다 우선하다

105

Anger restrained is wisdom gained.

Reference is made here to the wisdom of keeping anger in check. Note that "restrained" and "gained" rhyme here.

*Anger restrained is wisdom gained: 노염을 다스리면 지혜를 얻는다 / *Reference is made to X: X에 관하여 언급하고 있다 / *keep X in check: X를 억제하다

106

In the eyes of the lover, pockmarks are dimples.

They say "Love is blind." The proverb here touches on one of the consequences of love being blind.

*In the eyes of the lover: 사랑하는 이의 눈에는 / *pockmarks are dimples: 마맛자국도 보조개로 보인다 / *touch on the consequences of X: X의 결과에 대하여 언급하다

107

One of these days is none of these days.

This is a warning against procrastination, which is a thief of time. "(There is) no time like the present" makes a point similar to the one made here.

*One of these days is none of these days: 뒤로 미루어서 되는 일이 없다 / *procrastination: 지연, 지체 / *thief of time: 시간 도둑 / *(There is) no time like the present: 지금이 절호의 기회다, 지금 해야 한다

108

The used key is always bright.

Saying the same thing (from a negative perspective) is "Iron not used soon rusts." One implication for us is that we have to use our English on a regular basis if we are to keep it in good shape.

*negative perspective: negative point of view, 부정적인 견해 / *Iron not used soon rusts: 쇠도 사용하지 않으면 곧 녹이 슨다

109

Will is no skill.

The message here is that desire alone cannot get things done. "The spirit is willing, but the flesh is weak" also addresses the inadequacy of will.

*Will is no skill: 하고 싶은 일이라고 다 할 수 있는 것은 아니다 / *The spirit is willing: 욕망은 있다 / *the flesh is weak: 체력이 감당할 수 없다 / *address the inadequacy of will: 의지만으로는 부족하다는 점에 대하여 말하다

110

There is no place like home.

Expressing a similar sentiment are "East, west, home is best" and "Home is where the heart is."

*There is no place like home: 내 집이 최고다 / *East, west, home is best: 동서양 어디를 가던 내 집이 최고다 / *Home is where the heart is: 정든 곳이 집/고향이다, 정들면 고향이다

111

The doctor is often more to be feared than the disease.

Putting too much faith in doctors may sometimes do us more harm than good. Making a similar warning is "One doctor makes work for another."

*The doctor is often more to be feared than the disease: 의사를 병보다 무서워 해야 할 때가 자주 있다. / *put faith in X: X를 신뢰하다

112

Nurture is above nature.

The message here is that acquired capacity outweighs innate capacity. For some exceptional people, however, it may be the other way around. Mozart apparently is a case in point.

*acquired capacity: 후천적 능력 / *outweigh innate capacity: 선천적 능력보다 중요하다 / *the other way around: the opposite, 정반대 / *a case in point: 보기, 예

113

Leave is light.

"Leave means" "(asking) permission." And "light" means "easy." So what is said here is that asking permission is not that difficult. The implied message is that asking permission is good manners.

*Leave is light: 허락을 받는 것은 어렵지 않다 / *(asking) permission: 허락(을 요청하는 것) / *not that difficult: 그렇게 어렵지 않은

114

"They say so" is half a lie.

The point here is that rumor/gossip is often without foundation. Thus we would be well advised not to put too much store by the rumor/gossip mill.

*"They say so" is half a lie: "남들이 그렇게 말하더라"는 말의 반은 거짓말이다 / *be without foundation: 근거가 없다 / *would be well advised not to do X: X를 하지 않는 것이 좋다 / *put store by X: X를 높이 사다 / *the rumor/gossip mill: 소문/잡담 "방앗간"

115

Teaching of others teaches the teacher.

Indeed, one of the greatest joys of teaching is the joy of learning in the process. This point has been brought home to me again and again in my half-century as a teacher of English.

*in the process: 그 과정에서 / *be brought home to X: become clearly evident to X, X가 분명히 느끼게 되다 / *half century: 반세기

116

The boughs that bear most hang lowest.

The implication here is that great people tend to be modest and humble.

*The boughs that bear most: 열매가 가장 많이 열린 가지 / *tend to be modest and humble: 겸손한 경향이 있다

117

Do as you would be done by.

The implication here is: Treat people nice if you want them to treat you nice. Courtesy is indeed a two-way street. Don't you think?

*be done by: be done by other people, 다른 사람들의 대우를 받다 / *treat X nice: X를 좋게 대하다 / *Courtesy is a two-way street: 바른 예절은 쌍방통행이다

118

An Englishman's home is his castle.

The message here is that an Englishman is vigilantly protective of his privacy. Privacy is highly prized not just in England but also in much of the Western(nized) world.

*be vigilantly protective of X: X를 경계심을 풀지 않고 지키다 / *privacy: private space, 프라이버시, 사생활, 개인적인 공간 / *be highly prized: 중요시되다

119

Much would have more.

The focus here is on the insatiable nature of human greed. "The more you get, the more you want" makes the same point a bit more straightforwardly.

*Much would have more: 많이 가지면 더 많이 갖고 싶어 진다 / *The focus here is on X: 초점이 X에 맞추어져 있다 / *insatiable nature of human greed: 만족이 없는 인간 탐욕의 본성

120

People who live in glass houses shouldn't throw stones.

We must try and turn a blind eye to other people's shortcomings. For we all have weaknesses ourselves. "We all live in glass houses" delivers the same message.

*turn a blind eye to X: X를 눈감아 주다, X를 못 본척하다 / *shortcoming: weakness, 약점

121

The half is better than the whole.

Attention is called here to the value of the golden mean. Also referred to as the happy medium, the golden mean means the perfect middle course that avoids extremes.

*the golden mean: the happy medium, 중용, 중간 / *referred to as X: X라 불리는 (바) / *avoid extremes: 극단을 피하다

122

He that plants a tree plants for posterity.

The advice here is to take a long-term view of all serious undertakings such as the education of our children.

*plant for posterity: 후세를 위하여 심다 / *take a long-term view of X: X를 장기적 안목으로 보다 / *serious undertaking: 진지한 일, 중대한 과업

123

A little labor, much health.

A little physical work can go a long way in helping us stay healthy. So we might as well roll up our sleeves and put in some manual labor from time to time.

*labor: 노동 / *physical: 육체적인 / *might as well roll up our sleeves: 소매를 걷어붙이는 것이 좋을 것이다 / *put in some manual labor from time to time: 때때로 약간의 육체노동을 하다

124

Words cut more than swords.

The tongue is often so venomous that it can cause more pain than the sword. So we must always watch our tongue.

*sword: 칼, 검 / *venomous: 독이 가득한, 악의에 찬 / *watch one's tongue: 입 조심하다, 말조심하다

125

Woes unite foes.

Confronted with shared adversity, yesterday's adversaries often end up as today's allies. Incidentally, "woes" rhymes with "foes" here.

*Woes unite foes: 처지가 어렵게 되면 적들이라도 뭉치게 된다 / *Confronted with shared adversity: 같은 역경에 직면하면 / *adversary: 적 / *ally: 우군, 아군, 후원자

126

Something is better than nothing.

We should be grateful for what we currently have no matter how meager it may be. Besides, as they say, "The greatest wealth is contentment with a little."

*be grateful for X: X를 고마워하다 / *currently: 현재, 지금 / *meager: 미약한, 빈약한, 아주 소량의 / *contentment with X: X에 만족(함)

127

Old sins cast long shadows.

Bad deeds are not easily forgotten, are they? Given this message, we should take particular care not to let our deeds do harm to other people.

*cast a shadow: 그림자를 드리우다 / *deed: 행동 / *take particular care not to do X: X를 하지 않도록 각별히 주의하다

128

No reply is best.

This proverb says that no response is the best response when it comes to dealing with somebody who has done us wrong.

*No reply is best: 대꾸하지 않는 것이 상책이다 / *when it comes to dealing with X: X를 다룰 때 / *do X wrong: X에게 부당한 일을 하다

129

He that would have the fruit must climb the tree.

The message here is about the need to work our way to our goals however difficult that may be.

*He that would have the fruit: 과일을 먹고자 하는 사람(은) / *must climb the tree: 나무에 올라야 한다 / *work one's way to one's goal: 자기의 목표를 향하여 나아가다

130

A watched pot never boils.

We need to exercise extra patience when waiting for something to happen. The suggestion here is that impatience should be tossed out the window.

*A watched pot never boils: 끓기를 기다리고 있는 단지는 끓지 않는다 / *exercise extra patience: 특별한 인내심을 발휘하다 / *impatience should be tossed out the window: 성급함을 내버려야 한다

131

Measure is treasure.

This maxim is about the value of moderation. Note that "measure" rhymes with "treasure."

*Measure is treasure: 중용이 보배다 / *moderation: 중용, 절제

132

Be still, and have thy will.

The point here is that patience always pays off. Delivering a similar message is "Everything comes to him who waits."

*Be still, and have thy will: 잠자코 기다리고 있으면 뜻을 이룰 수 있다 /
*pay off: 좋은 결과를 가져 오다

133

The greatest wealth is contentment with a little.

Contentment with a little has always been my ticket to happiness. What about you? "Measure is treasure" and "Greedy eaters dig their graves with their teeth," remember?

*contentment with X: X에 대한 만족 / *a ticket to X: X에의 입장권 / *Greedy eaters dig their graves with their teeth: 너무 욕심 사납게 먹는 것은 제 손으로 제 무덤을 파는 것이다

134

Such beef, such broth.

Like "Garbage in, garbage out," the proverb here suggests that we cannot expect to get good output without good input.

*beef: 쇠고기 / *broth: 고깃국, 국물 / *Such beef, such broth: 그 쇠고기에 그 국물, 쇠고기가 좋아야 국물 맛이 좋다

135

No cross, no crown.

The road to success is always paved with suffering. So the wringer you are going through right now is not for nothing, right?

*No cross, no crown: 십자가의 고통이 없이는, 왕관도 없다. / *be paved with suffering: 고통으로 포장되어 있다 / *the wringer that you are going through: 지금 겪고 있는 고통 / *be not for nothing: 공연한 것이 아니다

136

Propsect is often better than possession.

The message here is that looking forward to getting something often trumps actually getting it. Being on a journey, for example, is often more fun than getting to its end point.

*Prospect is often better than possession: 흔히 기대감이 소유감보다 낫다 / *look forward to X: X를 학수고대하다 / *X trumps Y: X가 Y보다 낫다 / *be on a journey: 여행 중이다

137

He that wants health wants all.

Attention is called here to the overriding importance of our health. Bearing this in mind, let's always make sure that we are in the best of health.

*He that wants health wants all: 건강을 잃으면 모든 것을 잃는다 / *overriding: 절대적인, 압도적인 / *Bearing this in mind: 이것을 기억하면서

138

A little body often harbors a great soul.

The implication here is that a little body is often home to a great soul. Size is, indeed, not necessarily the major determinant of a person's worth.

*harbor a great soul: 위대한 영혼을 품고 있다 / *not necessarily X: not always X, 꼭 X가 아닌 / *determinant: 결정 요인

139

Things that are hard to come by are much set by.

The focus here is on the value of perseverance. With this message in mind, let's approach our study of English with a single-minded dedication.

*Things that are hard to come by: 얻기 힘든 것이 / *are much set by: 귀중한 것이다 / *With this message in mind: 이 점을 기억하여 / *approach X with a single-minded dedication: X를 전심전력으로 접근하다

140

We rise to great heights by a winding staircase.

Attributed to Francis Bacon (1561-1626), this maxim reminds us that achieving greatness requires a copious investment of patience and diligence.

*rise to great heights: 아주 높은 곳에 오르다 / *by a winding staircase: 꼬불꼬불한 계단을 거쳐서 / *Attributed to X: X가 말한 것으로 생각되는 바 / *copious investment: 아주 많은 투자

141

Iron not used soon rusts.

If not used often enough, your English, too, will soon rust. Try and use your English as much as you can. That's the best way to keep your English in shape.

*Iron not used soon rusts: 쇠는 사용하지 않으면 곧 녹이 슨다 / *Try and use your English: Try to use your English, 영어를 사용하도록 노력하라 / *keep X in shape: X를 좋은 상태로 유지하다

142

In the country of the blind, the one-eyed man is king.

A person of meager ability may stand out as a great leader where incompetents are in the majority. Greatness is thus often a matter of relative degree.

*a person of meager ability: 능력이 미미한 사람 / *stand out: 뛰어 나다 / *incompetents are in the majority: 무능력자들이 다수를 이루고 있다 / *a matter of relative degree: 상대적인 정도의 문제

143

No man is his craft's master the first day.

The point here is that getting to be a master of a trade takes a great deal of time and patience. Becoming a good speaker/writer of English is no exception.

*craft's master: a master of a trade, 일의 달인/장인 / *a great deal of X: 많은 X / *be no exception: 예외는 아니다

144

Less is more.

Wouldn't it be cool to spend less, rather than more? This witticism is grounded in the minimalist philosophy of life emerging throughout the world today.

*cool: 멋있는, 아주 좋은 / *witticism: 명언, 경구 / *be grounded in X: X에 근거를 두다 / *minimalist philosophy of life: 최소주의적인 인생철학 / *emerge: 나타나다, 대두하다

145

Tomorrow is another day.

We are told here to be optimistic. Hope for the future should keep us buoyant. Don't let today's problems bum you out too much.

*optimistic: 낙관적인 / *buoyant: 명랑한, 기운찬 / *bum X out: X를 실망시키다

146

The gown is his that wears it; the world, his that enjoys it.

It is not enough to just possess something. You have to be able to use it for your own good. Applied to our Holy Grail, which is mastery of English, the message here is that English is his that uses it.

*Applied to X: X에 적용시키면 / *our Holy Grail: 우리가 갈망하는 지상 목표

147

From a foolish judge, a quick sentence.

This maxim warns against rushing to judgment.

*sentence: 언도, 판결 / *This maxim warns against X: 이 금언은 X를 하지 말라는 경고이다 / *rush to judgment: 너무 성급하게 판단하다

148

Laws catch flies, but let hornets go free.

Laws are not always applied in a fair and consistent manner, are they? Sometimes, laws seem to discriminate against the powerless.

*Laws catch flies: 법은 (힘없는) 파리는 잡는다 / *but let hornets go free: 그러나 (힘센) 말벌은 놓아 준다 / *consistent: (시종)일관된 / *discriminate against X: X를 차별대우하다

149

Failing to prepare is preparing to fail.

Credited to the legendary John Wooden (b. 1911), a former UCLA basketball coach, this saying focuses on the value of preparation in everything we do.

*Failing to prepare is preparing to fail: 준비를 하지 않음은 실패를 준비함이다 / *credited to X: attributed to X, X가 한 말로 전해지는 (바) / *legendary: 전설적인

150

Flow of words is not always flow of wisdom.

It says to always choose our words carefully. "Deliver your words not by number but by weight" offers another way of making a similar point.

*Deliver your words: 말을 하다 / *not by number but by weight: (단어의) 숫자로가 아니라 그 무게로

151

He who rides a tiger is afraid to dismount.

We must persevere until we bring whatever is underway to a conclusion. Making about the same point is "In for a penny, in for a pound."

*dismount: (동물의 등에서) 내려 오다 / *persevere: 참고 견디다 / *under-way: 진행중인 / *In for a penny, in for a pound: 기왕에 시작한 일은 끝장을 낸다

152

In doing, we learn.

The wisdom implied here is applicable to our study of English. The best way to learn the language may be to actually use it.

*be applicable to X: X에 적용될 수 있다

153

Thrift is a great revenue.

Emphasis is placed here on the virtue of frugality. Although the primary focus is on money matters, this proverb does have implications beyond mere economics.

*Thrift is a great revenue: 검약이 큰 소득이다 / *frugality: 검약, 근검절약 / *beyond mere economics: 단순한 경제를 넘어서

154

Dumb dogs are dangerous.

They say that dogs that do not bark tend to be more dangerous than those that do. The same is apparently true of people, too. Those who are silent may pose more of a problem than those who aren't.

*Dumb dogs are dangerous: 소리 없는 개가 위험하다 / *bark: 짖다 / *pose a problem for X: X에게 문제가 되다

155

The hunchback does not see his own hump, but sees his companion's.

No one is infallible and thus we should refrain from being too critical of other people. "People who live in glass houses shouldn't throw stones" makes a similar point.

*hunchback: 꼽추, 곱사등이 / *hump: 곱사등, 불룩 솟은 혹 / *companion: 동료, 친구 / *infallible: 오류가 없는, 잘못으로부터 자유로운

156

The cat would eat fish and would not wet her feet.

The reference here is to the cunning cat trying to catch fish without going into the water. Shouldn't the cat accept the inconvenience of getting her feet wet if she is to catch fish for a meal?

*The reference here is to X: 여기 언급은 X에 관한 것이다 / *cunning: 약삭빠른, 교활한 / *inconvenience: 불편 / *if she is to catch fish for a meal: 끼니로 먹기 위해 생선을 잡으려면

Key-word index

The reference is to the maxim number.

초판1쇄 인쇄 2009년 2월 23일
초판1쇄 발행 2009년 3월 1일

지은이 | 박남식
펴낸이 | 박남식
펴낸곳 | 국제영어대학원대학교 출판부
등록 | 2003년 8월 28일(제 17-362호)
주소 | 서울특별시 강동구 성내3동 449-11
전화 | (02) 6477-5105
팩스 | (02) 6477-5111
이메일 | press@igse.ac.kr
홈페이지 | www.igse.ac.kr
ISBN 978-89-956324-2-0 02740

* 책 값은 뒤표지에 있습니다.